LEAH
HERO FOR JESUS

The Real-Life Story of Leah Sharibu

Told by Leah's Family and Friends

Compiled by Dr. Gloria Samdi-Puldu
and Peter Fretheim

LEAH
HERO FOR JESUS

The Real-Life Story of Leah Sharibu

Told by Leah's Family and Friends

Compiled by Dr. Gloria Samdi-Puldu
and Peter Fretheim

Cover Design: Lee Cantelon
Typesetting: Ocreative

Editors:
Becca Lubbert, Rejoice Puldu, Monday Ogbe, Heather Ricks,
Adriana Myland, Claire McKeown, The Challengers,
Philip Begho, Bayo Alabi, Kyle Abts, Barbara Rosseland,
John Kennedy, Hannah Fretheim and others.

First paperback edition April 2021

Images by Lee Cantelon, Kyle Abts, Gloria Samdi-Puldu, and Peter Fretheim

ISBN 978-0-578-97950-2 (paperback)

ISBN 978-978-905-488-6 (e-mob)

ISBN 978-978-905- 489-3 (e-pub)

Disclaimer:

The material in this publication is of the nature of general comment only, and does not represent professional advice. It is not intended to provide specific guidance for particular circumstances and it should not be relied on as the basis for any decision to take action or not take action on any matter which it covers. Readers should obtain professional advice where appropriate, before making any such decision. To the maximum extent permitted by law, the author and publisher disclaim all responsibility and liability to any person, arising directly or indirectly from any person taking or not taking action based on the information in this publication

DEDICATION

*We dedicate this book to Leah for the amazing
act of courage that she displayed, and to Jesus her Lord
for leading and guiding her through this terrible ordeal.*

We will never be the same because of her story!

ACKNOWLEDGMENT

We wish to acknowledge those who made this book possible:

First, to Leah's parents for raising her to be a hero, for helping us start the LEAH Foundation (*Leah-Foundation.org*), for their firsthand account of her life and connecting us to so many other eyewitnesses.

For all of those willing to tell us the story — even though it could cost them, as some don't want the story to be told.

Lee Cantelon and Microboard USA for helping us create the LEAH Foundation, as well as supporting vital work among girls and women in Nigeria. Lee also helped in gathering some of these eyewitness accounts and he personally took many of the pictures contained in this book.

The LEAH Foundation leadership committee for their time and effort to help Leah, her family, her best friends, and others that are in some form of "captivity."

All those listed on page III and others who helped in one way or another. We had a lot of great teamwork on this project and that is shown by the excellent end result.

Kyle Abts for his leadership in helping to set up the LEAH Foundation, as well as his tireless efforts to advocate for Leah around the world. He was also able to help arrange appearances of Rebecca Sharibu and Gloria Samdi-Puldu before the United States Senate, House of Representatives, as well as the House of Lords in the United Kingdom!

Dr. Doug Green and his wife, Kelley, who graciously funded the creation and publication of this book. Due to their generosity, we will be able to use all proceeds from this book to help girls and women like Leah.

CONTENTS

FROM THE AUTHORS

M Y FAMILY AND I ARE MISSIONARIES WITH SIM (Serving In Mission) in Nigeria and have been serving here since 1999. Leah's amazing story has greatly impacted my life. I am not the same because of her. All the work we are doing to help women and girls in need is dedicated to her. At the age of only 14, she single-handedly stood up to Boko Haram—the deadliest terrorist organization in the world! I am so challenged by her brave example and constantly ask myself what I would do if the terrorists came for me. She stood for Jesus because He is her Hero. Now, due to this extraordinary act of courage, she has become my hero and the hero of a nation!

– Peter Fretheim

W HEN PETER FRETHEIM ASKED ME TO BE THE president of the LEAH Foundation (Leah-Foundation.org), I prayed and sought God's will. Accepting this position to advocate for Leah's release and to help other women and girls like her has been the most rewarding experience of my life. The LEAH Foundation is the only organization in the world officially authorized to represent Leah. The two of us started this Nigerian NGO (nongovernmental organization) along with Leah's parents and other committed individuals, including the president of Evangelical Church Winning All (ECWA). ECWA is Leah's church and is one of the largest denominations in Africa.

This story is told by eyewitnesses who knew her and experienced her life firsthand. In some cases, we have withheld their names to protect their identities.

Leah is my hero and as you read her story, my guess is she will become one of yours as well.

– Dr. Gloria Samdi-Puldu
(Lecturer of Political Science at the
University of Jos, Plateau State, Nigeria)

FOREWORD

T HE STORY OF LEAH SHARIBU IS A STORY OF GOD'S incredible manifestation of His grace and election, which transforms an ordinary person (*irrespective of his age, gender, family background, place of birth and status*) into an extraordinary being who shows exceptional courage and uncommon faith in Christ in the face of the brutality that characterizes humanity.

Leah becomes a symbol of the Christian faith, loudly expressing that the powers of hell can never subdue the Kingdom of our Lord and Savior, Jesus Christ.

The book, **Leah: Hero for Jesus**, compiled by the authors and as told by Leah's family and friends, should be read by every Christian, especially children and teenagers.

I have no doubt that the story told here will inspire readers to repent. A sense of godliness will ultimately humble the unbelieving world to come to the feet of our Lord and Savior, Jesus Christ.

Of course this is not the end of Leah's story, as we prayerfully await her release from captivity.

We recommend this book without any reservation!

God bless you,

Pastor E. A. Adeboye
General Overseer (The Redeemed Christian Church of God)

PREFACE

"We must celebrate
the exception of one who said 'no.'
Just as Nelson Mandela said 'no.'
When Leah said 'no,'
she spoke for all of us.
Her torch must not be dimmed."

– Wole Soyinka
Nobel Prize for Literature Winner

Her Torch Must Not Be Dimmed

O N FEB. 19, 2018, A VIOLENT AND DESPICABLE ACT SET *in motion a sequence of circumstances that would eventually attract the attention of the world and bring one 14-year-old girl's name to the lips of political leaders, human rights activists, Christian communities, and even a Nobel Prize-winning author. Until then, the violent kidnapping of children, primarily schoolgirls, by terrorist groups had been reported widely in the international press, but the victims had remained anonymous. Those abducted were referred to as a number, a tragic statistic without face or name. Then there was Leah.*

On that Monday in February, Leah Sharibu, along with 110 other girls ages 11-19, were taken hostage by Boko Haram. Her abduction took place around 5:30 p.m. from the Government Girls' Science and Technical College (GGSTC) in Dapchi, Yobe State, in northeast Nigeria, 170 miles from Chibok. That's where Boko Haram's strategy of kidnapping girls as an act of terror and demoralization had come to the world's attention after they took 276 girls hostage in 2014.

It is still difficult to imagine that a 14-year old girl could have the courage to do what Leah did, given the choice of freedom or captivity. Without her courage, the plight of hundreds and thousands of children being held hostage by Boko Haram today might have receded into oblivion, much like the terrorists and their captives disappear into the wilds of the Lake Chad Basin and Sambisa Forest.

But Leah said "no." That single-syllable word sounded a bell that has resonated across thousands of miles, and penetrated barriers of culture, ignorance, and apathy. Leah's "no" echoed in the hearts and minds of thousands, then hundreds of thousands, and now millions around the world.

Four weeks after the Dapchi kidnapping, on March 16, Boko Haram released 104 of the girls taken hostage (five had died on the initial journey). Those freed were dropped off from nine vehicles. Many will recall seeing the photographs of the girls, all dressed in plain brown hijabs, sitting on the ground in a group, many still in shock. These "Dapchi girls" brought with them not only accounts of the horrors of their ordeal, but the story of their friend Leah's refusal to deny her faith, an act that had forced them to leave her behind. The news of Leah's refusal to submit to her captors spread rapidly. A few days later, The Guardian and Agence France-Presse broke the story of "Leah Sharibu, the teenage girl not released along with the other hostages because she refused to convert to Islam."

In May 2018, I traveled to Nigeria to spend time with Peter and Miriam Fretheim and their mission. This was my third visit to support their efforts through the mission's program at Microboard that supports relief efforts to women and orphans, many of them victims of the crisis afflicting the people of the northern Nigerian states. By then, Leah had been captive 12 weeks. Peter asked me if I would be willing to travel north to meet Leah's parents, Nathan and Rebecca, and document their appeals for Leah's release. If I did, it would be the first video recording of its kind, and hopes were that it would be seen by those in a position to advocate on her behalf, including the Trump administration in Washington, D. C., and human rights agencies in the United States. Immediately I agreed.

View the video that was recorded at that time:
https://www.youtube.com/watch?v=fhBbNqQe5ow

Awakened from Our Sleep

SOMETIMES IN LIFE THERE ARE MOMENTS, USUALLY *unforeseen, when you are forced to confront yourself honestly and without pretense. Such moments of clarity reveal truths about who you are, what you believe, how far you are willing to go to do the right thing. Such moments often take place in a crisis or in an unexpected encounter. They can be unsettling, and should be so. Complacency allows wrongs and evils to exist. We need to be shaken. Leah's story has that power to awaken us from our sleep.*

Traveling north to meet Leah's parents took many hours. Because of the death threats and security risks, Nathan and Rebecca traveled to the undisclosed location in two separate vehicles as an added precaution. Nathan served in the Nigerian police force, so he knew the drill, and they had carefully planned their routes. The day dragged

*on, but in the late afternoon we received news that the meeting
would go ahead as planned. We loaded our van and set out for the
predetermined safe house. After passing through nearly a dozen
military checkpoints, we reached our destination. Tall iron gates
opened from the inside and we entered the compound without slowing
down. An hour or so later, two more vehicles arrived, their windows
darkened, Rebecca in one, Nathan in the other.*

*Being face to face with Leah's mother and father was to confront
the emotional fallout of terrorism, the toll it takes on the families
who have lost a family member — God-forbid a child — to these
systematic acts of violence. The tension in the room was palpable,
the curtains having been drawn even though a tall concrete wall
shrouded the house. Not a breath of air stirred. As if in reaction to the
semi-darkness, our voices dropped to near whispers. We exchanged
greetings.*

*I remember feeling awkward, me being from the West with a passport
and plane ticket in my bag that could carry me away to safety and
comfort at any moment. Everything about me, every detail of my
life, stood in such contrast to the two people with me in that room.
What did I know, or how could I ever grasp the suffering their lives
had experienced, even before their daughter's kidnapping? The gap
of privilege or the lack of privilege between us was great. How could
I adequately empathize with what they endured? Only God's Spirit,
the Holy Spirit spoken of in the Bible, could help bridge this kind of
emotional disparity. The bridge presented itself as my heart melted
and my eyes suddenly filled with tears. All I could say was, "God loves
you, We love you."*

*Together we sat down. First Rebecca and then Nathan spoke, their
subdued voices barely audible even in the hushed room. They spoke of
the pain they felt, a pain plainly visible on their faces, as if they lived
through those first terrible hours once again. I wondered then if they
had known even an hour of relief from such emotional torture since
that terrible day. Rebecca spoke of how she had heard the news first
and had rushed to the school in the morning. Surrounded by other
frantic parents, she had wept and begged school officials and the police
to find her daughter. The reality that their children were already far
away and prisoners of the terrorists was more than she could bear.
Together with the other mothers she emptied herself of tears, even as
she tried to comfort others. Leah's classmates had, by then, confirmed
that she had been one of the girls taken hostage.*

*Seventeen months after interviewing Leah's parents, I met Rebecca
Sharibu for a second time. She had come to the United States to
speak before the U.S. Senate on Capitol Hill, traveling with Dr. Gloria
Samdi-Puldu, president of the LEAH Foundation (Leah-Foundation.
org). Though so many months had passed, the pall of grief was still
evident in Rebecca's face.*

*"God help me to be discomforted," I prayed then. I hope to pray that
whenever I think of Leah, Rebecca, Nathan, Leah's brother Donald, or
the Dapchi girls being looked after by Gloria, Miriam, Peter, and their
team. "Don't let me forget to feel some part of their pain, or get too far
removed from their hurting."*

*If one member of the body suffers, all suffer together. And if one
member of the body is honored, then all rejoice together (1 Corinthians
12:26). The Bible teaches this in the apostle Paul's letter to some early
Christians.*

In Nigeria today, uncounted thousands are suffering. Christians and non-Christians alike grieve because of the pain and loss they have experienced as a result of the ongoing insurgency. We may never fully appreciate or understand what they are going through, but we can pray that God will help us feel their suffering on a personal level and in doing so, be motivated to love more and find more ways to help.

Leah's courage is relentless. It inspires hope and courage to many, even as it has the power to convict. She has become the face of the victims of the degradation and abuse women and girls experience in Africa and elsewhere around the world. Leah's stand for Christ proposes a challenge to us all. Meeting her mother and father is something I cannot escape from or ignore. I can only pray that God makes it possible to keep that moment present and real, and that I never fail to hurt for them, until the day Leah and all of the girls in captivity are released. I will seek to do my part so that her "no" will never be in vain. How about you?

— Lee Cantelon (Microboard USA)

Lee (middle) with Nathan and Rebecca in Northern Nigeria

I ♥ LEAH

I ♥ LEAH

young girls across Nigeria write lette to their sister, Leah...

1

A CLASSMATE'S ACCOUNT
Life in Dapchi

IT IS AMAZING HOW ONE MOMENT CAN BE SO NORMAL, yet the next can be so life-changing.

Loud gunshots ring out! Everyone runs to hide. *More gunshots!* Oh no, is this really happening? We need to get out of here. A million things run through my mind. Is it Boko Haram? Where should I run? How do we get to safety?

With sweat running down my face and body, and the adrenaline kicking in, I gasp for air while trying to escape from the men firing machine guns. They are wearing black clothes and turbans. I sprint across the dirt, dodging bullets. Sticks prick my feet. Not giving much thought to where I should go, all I can do is charge ahead. Hundreds of screaming girls run frantically out of their dormitories heading for the school gate.

What's happening? Where is the principal? Where are the schoolteachers? Are the police or military coming to protect us? The fear of Boko Haram attacking is actually coming true! What's going to happen? All I can do is pray that God will protect us. "Help, O God! Please help us! Please, I beg you, Lord!"

I grew up in Dapchi, a small town in Yobe State, in the northeastern part of Nigeria. Before terror struck, it seemed like any other place in Northern Nigeria and was relatively peaceful. Temperatures regularly rose above 100 degrees Fahrenheit, and because of the desert location, the sun would beat down on us and form beads of perspiration on our foreheads.

Men gathered under the trees outside their homes and at the village center to stay cool from the scorching heat, while women and children sat on mats spread outside their rooms but within the compounds. Just like in Bible times, dirt from the dusty ground covered our feet.

Farming and raising animals are the main ways of making a living in Dapchi. During the dry season, nothing grows due to the harsh weather. The rainy season brings some relief, but it never lasts long enough. At least that's the way it feels when the dry heat returns to erase all thought of the cool rain.

We only have two seasons here: the dry season, which lasts from September through May, and the rainy season, which only lasts a few months in between. Because of the harsh conditions, hard-working parents dream of giving their children a different life. So they try to send us to primary school, and when elementary education is completed, our parents often sacrifice everything to send us to secondary school, which is often a boarding school. Locals hope that a proper education will result in more career opportunities. Simply put, education is seen as the way out of the hard life of farming and rearing sheep and goats. What parent doesn't want something better for his or her child?

That life in Dapchi no longer exists. The place is located near the border between Nigeria and Niger. It still has scant rainfall. From the rising of the sun to its setting, the same routine of farming and raising animals continues, as well as the routine of selling meager supplies and sitting under trees to escape the heat.

What makes that way of life obsolete is the fact that an unbelievable terror became the dividing line between going to bed one night in the past like normal, then waking up the next day into the present reality of a continuing nightmare.

This shift happened while I was away at school. How I long now for a return of that old normal life!

I was one of the favored ones able to attend the boarding school. It is the Government Girls' Science and Technical College, simply called GGSTC Dapchi. It is where girls from the surrounding villages are sent to gain an education. It's a secondary school, running from junior to senior levels, that is, from 7th to 12th grade. It's really the only quality middle/high school for many miles around.

I cannot describe what school is like in other places because I've been nowhere else. I woke up every day at GGSTC to a familiar routine of prayers and chores before school. Our stomachs rumbled through the first few classes as we waited until break time to have our first meal. At the end of classes, we had homework to do.

I assume one of the main differences between my school and schools elsewhere is that at GGSTC Dapchi we are extremely relational. We focus on things that bring us together, such as religious activities and clubs. Our attention is not on the busyness of life, or social media or computer games, which we can't even access.

Because we were together, the chores and rumbling stomachs and homework were all bearable. The only interruption to this simple routine of school life was when teachers did not show up for their classes. This happened often. They simply decided to not come to school. We were supposed to have eight classes during the day, but sometimes we had only two.

An unpleasantness existed in our simple routine, though undetectable in any photograph of me. A picture only showed smiles, laughter, and usual emotions of a typical secondary schoolgirl. No photo would illustrate my Christian faith.

Being a Christian in a school with only a few other Christians made life difficult.

Dapchi is a predominantly Muslim town where only about 10 percent of the residents are Christians. There are only four small churches in the Dapchi area, with each congregation numbering less than 30 people. The pressure to deny one's faith and to live as a Muslim starts at a young age. Generally, in Yobe State it is hard for Christian children to receive any formal education.

Christian adults often are overlooked for jobs or leadership positions at the local or state levels due to religious discrimination. The persecution is real, and evident on a daily basis. However, this kind of everyday persecution pales in comparison to what we were about to face.

Life had been generally peaceful in Dapchi until 2009, when Boko Haram began attacks in the neighboring state of Borno. In 2014, the tension and fear among inhabitants of Dapchi rose to a new height when 276 young schoolgirls — girls just like us at GGSTC — were kidnapped from their secondary school in Chibok, Borno State.

It was too close!

Though some of the girls later were rescued, many died, some of them killed as suicide bombers. An estimated 99 girls are still missing.

The world paused to grieve momentarily, but for us at Dapchi where the atrocity happened right next door, we are still grieving. Our lives have never been the same. Worse, Chibok has been attacked several more times and no one seems willing or able to stop the terrorists.

We live with the realization that Boko Haram could cross state lines at any time and overturn our lives in unimaginable ways. Most mornings we wake up wondering if this is the day we must face the terror of Boko Haram.

Are we safe? Will we meet a violent death? Will our lives be overthrown by maiming and destruction? An anxious knot of impending doom lives in our stomachs, telling us that it is only a matter of time before something horrific happens.

The constant weight of this terror forced some families, especially Christian ones, out of Yobe State to areas where the threat of Boko Haram is less severe. Those who remain try to continue normal daily life to earn what little money they can to feed their families, though fear is their constant companion.

There is nothing inherently wrong in the decision to leave or stay. Both have consequences. The normal routine of life, no matter how hard, gives comfort, and for those of us who stay, it is just how we chose to take care of our families in order to survive.

I wish I could say that with the passing of each day, and each month, and each year, the thought of Boko Haram and the havoc they had carried out at Chibok slowly faded. It did not. As schoolgirls, we all remained terrified that what happened at Chibok would happen to us.

In fact, Boko Haram left letters at our school and the house of the chief of Dapchi, threatening to attack. The town wondered if the threat would actually be carried out or if it was merely meant to scare us.

Then it happened.

That day put the faith of the Dapchi community to the utmost test, especially for the Sharibu family.

2

SIYONA'S ACCOUNT
Who is Leah?

WHO IS LEAH Sharibu? As a classmate, family friend, and fellow church member of hers, I can give plenty of facts about Leah. They would describe the story of a 14-year-old girl who loved to sing and play handball, who enjoyed high-jump athletic events.

She served as president of the school's Fellowship of Christian Students and had been a natural leader from early childhood. Most unusually, she was even selected to be a school prefect, an important leadership position that rarely went to outspoken Christian girls like her.

As a firm believer in Jesus, she always stood up against the persecution and mistreatment that Christians had to endure in school. But this only paints part of the picture.

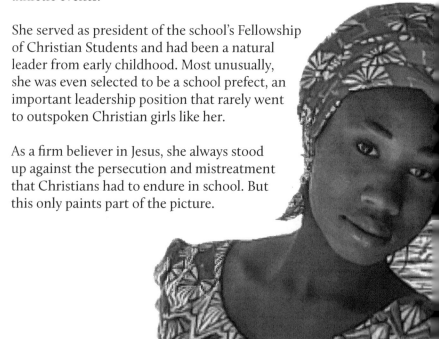

You might still view her as an ordinary girl. That would be totally wrong, because Leah was anything but ordinary.

Leah grew up with the kind of faith that could withstand the greatest trials. Even adults could learn from the type of faith she possessed. Another friend of hers described Leah as "a girl whose faith was so strong that she was willing to act as Christ showed us in the Bible." As Leah continually stood up to the barrage of insults from non-Christian schoolmates, she taught the less strong among us how to be brave.

Persecution is nothing people seek out themselves. As Christians living in Dapchi, we experienced day-to-day persecution. The name-calling, the mocking of our faith, being overlooked for benefits, and being misunderstood all became the usual pattern we had to endure.

Our Sunday School teacher explained that just like Jesus suffered on earth, we also must experience suffering at the hands of unbelievers. Like Jesus was different, we, too, would have to show the world by our conduct and attitudes that we were different. This lesson proved particularly important on the numerous occasions that we experienced the threat of harm.

Leah fully understood this truth and it helped her live differently from most. She befriended not only Christians, but Muslims as well. She was well respected and feared nothing. The trials and hardships she suffered seemed only to strengthen her. If not for her example, I doubt I would have been able to endure what was to come.

I remember a particular experience I had at the place where the townspeople usually went to grind grain. When it was my turn after waiting a long time in the line, the Muslim man who operated the grinding machine decided to charge me a price much higher than he charged others. I asked why, and he called me names, insulted my faith, and ordered me to leave.

Leah arrived just as I protested angrily. In her usual way, she told me not to let the matter bother me. She reminded me that my response as a Christian had to be different. I was so upset. I wanted God to strike the man — and all who took sides with him — dead.

Leah insisted that I had to forgive him, for he and the others against me didn't know what they were doing. In a calm and gentle manner, she asked him what he wanted for grinding my beans, and she paid him his fee in advance from her money. As the man set to work, he scowled at me and snarled, "God saved you!"

Leah's strength and trust in the Lord helped us all to be better witnesses of Christ to those around us.

Her unshakable faith started at home. Nathan and Rebecca Sharibu adopted Leah when she was young, as Nathan's brother Irmiya Sharibu was killed in a motorcycle accident. The Sharibu family was a normal Christian family growing up in northern Nigeria. Like others of the faith, they felt the tension of being in the minority. Leah's parents taught her and her brother, Donald, stories from a Bible translated into Hausa. What a treasure to have God's Word written in one's own language!

Leah and Donald Sharibu

The Sharibus took part in family devotions and attended church together, learning the importance of reading and memorizing Bible verses. Because of this early family exposure to Christ, Leah and Donald accepted Jesus as their Lord and Savior at early ages, understanding that the Christian God is the only true God.

Leah had a real heart for the Lord and wanted to follow his commands and live like Jesus, as taught in the Bible.

From the Sharibu household, God's love spread to those around them. Leah's parents were shining lights in their community. They were dedicated to making friends and living in harmony with their Muslim neighbors. God's Word shaped and transformed their lives, teaching them how to navigate life as Christians in a predominantly Muslim community.

As I write out Leah's life one memory at a time, the extent of God's sovereignty becomes more and more clear. In a society where Christians are often bypassed for privileges, Leah's father worked as a police officer, which is a federal government job. He worked hard to provide for his family to give his children an education that could help them have a good life. Donald enrolled in a boarding school outside Dapchi because no such school for boys existed in Dapchi. Leah attended the same girls' secondary school as I did.

Though Leah may not exactly be like Esther of the Bible in the sense that she was not placed in an earthly royal position, it does feel as though God placed her in our lives "for such a time as this." I have no doubt that the person I have become would have been entirely different without her.

As life continued in Dapchi, Boko Haram drew closer. It is hard to push terror out of one's mind when terrorists are nearby. Leah's father spent long periods away from his family because as a police officer he had to be stationed in other cities and states. When he heard that Boko Haram attacks had drawn closer to Dapchi, he stepped up prayers, asking his Christian associates to join him to intercede for the protection of his family.

For Leah and her mother, living in the heart of the news and rumors, what could they do but pray? They prayed and trusted God and continued to be a light in the darkness that surrounded them.

Prayer alone can give us strength and hope during a hard season of life. Our connection with our Heavenly Father empowers us. Leah led many school activities, including our prayer group. We prayed about many things, but because Boko Haram was a daily topic of conversation, we never stopped praying for protection from them.

As I think of how fervently we prayed and of the reality that many others prayed for us, I understand another lesson that God teaches us. In a supernatural way, He prepares our hearts for whatever difficulties we must face.

So again I ask, who is Leah?

Leah is different from other people. Leah is so patient and tolerant. I cannot help remembering what she often told us about name-calling. She said when we are insulted by people, it is because they want to provoke us to anger; we mustn't let them succeed by giving in to anger.

I also remember how she helped us build a strong prayer habit. Whenever our Muslim schoolmates went to their prayers, she encouraged us to also come together to pray. Leah was bold and courageous in her faith. Every time she and I and our friends Comfort and Vashti discussed what we would do if ever attacked, Leah adamantly declared that we should never deny Jesus, no matter the harm done to us!

She said that even if the terrorists threatened to take our lives, we should never deny the One we loved, Jesus. Little did we know that God was preparing her heart for the ultimate test about to come.

3

PATIENCE'S ACCOUNT
Amazing Courage

I WAS LEAH'S SCHOOLMATE, ONE YEAR AHEAD OF HER in class. As fellow Christians, we were always together in fellowship groups, Sunday services, evening devotions in our dormitories, and numerous spontaneous prayer times.

On the Sunday evening of the day before the attack, all the Christian students gathered in Leah's dormitory for normal devotions. As we chatted after the devotion before bedtime, Leah's best friend in school, Liatu, brought up the issue of Boko Haram.

As if Leah knew something would happen, she asked all of us the question: "If you were taken away by Boko Haram tonight and they asked you to renounce your faith in Jesus, would you do it?" Some replied they would, if that would help get them released, claiming they would later come back to the faith.

But Leah boldly said, "That is what I'll never do, no matter what happens!" She then told us the story of an elder in a nearby church who had recently been captured by Boko Haram. The man agreed to renounce his faith and convert to Islam when ordered to do so. Upon being released, he happily started off, but the Boko Haram leader raised his gun and shot him to death.

Leah confronted us. "Did the man save his life by renouncing Jesus? No, he suffered great loss." As we stared in shock, she added, "This is the reason I'll never renounce the Lord." She urged us that fateful night to always stand for Christ, no matter the trial. She said in Hausa, *"Yesu ya taimake mu"* (May Jesus help us all.) We all answered in Hausa, *"Amin"* (Amen).

After the talk, she asked us to pray one more time before going to bed, and we did.

Leah's courage, words of exhortation, and strong faith in Christ made me wonder if she was really a young girl. I must admit that I could not in a thousand years be as courageous as Leah. She was the only Christian in school who fittingly challenged the other students and teachers who called us infidels and other names. Her patience and calm demeanor ensured that anger never got the best of her. Rather, she sensibly explained to her accusers that Christians serve a Living God and aren't infidels.

Often when Leah wasn't there to respond calmly, a heated quarrel resulted. Or if we tried to remain silent, our antagonists would say, "Now you'll probably go and tell your warrior Leah about it," and they would mock us.

Leah was strong for us, and she pointed us to our ultimate warrior: Jesus Christ.

When the girls who had been taken captive with Leah came back and described how she fearlessly stood up to the terrorists, I immediately remembered how she said she would never renounce her faith no matter what happened. She had not uttered empty words.

Leah proved to be courage in human form!

On Monday, the day of the attack, I learned that my friend Comfort was sick, so I planned to see her after the evening prep. But then I heard gunshots and ran for safety to the nearby staff quarters. There was no space for me in the first house because other students already had raced to fill it up.

I then fled to another house, where a teacher's wife who lived there took some of us in and locked us in a room for safety. We sat there trembling in silence. A couple of Boko Haram soldiers came to the front door demanding to know if students were hiding in the house. The woman said no. They smashed the door down to search and marched to our door to try and open it.

The woman said in Hausa, "*Dakin Mallam ne kumayafita da makullinsa*" (That is my husband's room and he left home with the key). They believed her and went off to search for other students. I find it incredible to have escaped. It turned out Leah was the only Christian student taken that day. I have often wondered if this stemmed from her being the only one of us who was prepared.

not just refuge, but a palace

"Imagine yourself as a living house. God comes in to rebuild that house. You thought you were being made into a decent little cottage: but He is building a palace. He intends to come and live in it Himself." C. S. Lewis (Mere Christianity)

Patience

4

REBECCA'S ACCOUNT #1
A Mother's Prayer

*Dear God, please protect my husband while he is away.
Grant him safety, especially since Boko Haram is active in the
areas where he serves. I also lift up Donald and Leah to You.
Thank You for my precious children and thank You, too, for
so generously providing us with the means to give them an
education. I pray that they will remain close to You while they
are away at school, and that their classmates will see who You
are through them. Continue to draw us closer to You, and
protect us all. In Jesus' name. Amen.*

Leah's Family Compound in Dapchi

I ALWAYS BEGIN MY MORNING READING GOD'S WORD and praying before I do any chores or go to work. This is what gives me the strength I need. However, on the Monday Boko Haram attacked, I did not know how important my devotions with God would be. I so needed His power that day, more than ever before.

As I started off to fetch water, the day seemed just like any other Monday morning. I drew water from the well and then spent time cleaning the house and preparing the household meal before heading off to start a day of teaching at school.

I am a teacher at a primary school, not too far from where my daughter Leah attended secondary school. We had her boarding there so she could concentrate on her studies, and with God's help, one day gain a better life for herself.

The day moved on and school went smoothly. When I returned home, I had a meal and then went out to spend the late afternoon chatting with my neighbors, as usual.

Evening is always the time I enjoy most. It's a relatively cool time of the day, and being a communal people in Dapchi, many residents come out to enjoy each other's company. I love spending time with my neighbors and catching up on the news of the day.

Leah's House

That Monday I sat out in front of my house, a normal activity if I don't go over to my neighbor's compound.

It was a peaceful evening. Chatter and laughter rang through the village. We at Dapchi are generally a contented and happy people, grateful for the simple things of life. I often close my eyes and look back on the peaceful times we enjoyed. I long for this, but it does not seem possible. I so wish I could go back to a time before the horror of that terrible evening.

One moment I talked with a friend who came to visit. The next moment, gunfire shattered our conversation. Chatter and laughter instantly ceased. Instead, chaos broke out, and in wild panic people raced for the bush with their children. My visitor disappeared.

In this region, whenever there is a Boko Haram invasion, people flee to the bush or nearby mountains to hide because often the terrorists set houses ablaze, burning everyone alive in their own homes.

Gunfire!

More gunfire in the distance!

I could not tell the exact origin of the shooting. Was this Boko Haram? *What on earth was happening?* Was Boko Haram attacking Dapchi? Was my worst nightmare coming true?

With my heart beating frantically, I leapt from my bench and dashed into the neighboring house.

"*What's happening?*" I demanded of my neighbor.

She trembled. "It must be Boko Haram!"

The gunshots continued. Crying and screaming, confused people ran all around us.

I already knew in my heart this must be Boko Haram. Even so, I really didn't want to voice such thoughts out loud.

"We must run!" my neighbor breathlessly muttered.

I shook my head. "I can't! I need to find my Leah! I must go to her school and find her!"

"Wait!" My friend reached for me, "You mustn't go there! We don't know from which side they're attacking. You must stay here. We need to stick together."

We huddled together in her house. I held my breath and prayed. The gunfire and turmoil continued, ringing through the evening.

"*Dear God, we need you more than ever before,*" I prayed. "*Please watch over the people of Dapchi and protect our children from harm. We know that you are bigger and more powerful than any man. May these men who want to do us harm encounter you and your love. Please bring us peace. In the mighty name of Jesus. Amen!*"

Suddenly, calm returned. The gunfire stopped. My mind raced to my daughter.

What about Leah? What about Leah's school? Was the school attacked? Did they harm or take any of the girls?

5

COMFORT'S ACCOUNT
Terror

TRAGEDY CAN BECOME LODGED INTO YOUR MEMORY as unwanted debris, making you remember everything about a moment, no matter how hard you try to forget it. When you least expect, the pieces become dangerously infected. It is all that you think about.

This is what happened to me. Details of images, smells, and conversations of that Monday became frozen in my mind. They hold me captive and make me relive the day again and again.

But there are two specific memories of that day that have clung to me like no other.

Leah at a younger age

The first is a comforting one, the thought of Leah's caring heart. This is what I hold on to when I try to conquer all other haunting thoughts. Leah always put the needs of others before her own, and on that day, she cared for me. I will never forget that. Boarding school is tough, especially our sort in the north. Good friends are hard to come by, particularly those who stand by you when you aren't at your best.

When I think back to that day, I can only describe it as ordinary: sunny and hot. Cleaning our dormitories and their surroundings has to be completed in the morning before classes start. However, on this day I felt very sick. Because of my illness, Leah reached out to me in kindness and love.

I felt too ill to attend any classes that day, though I knew there might be homework. The sounds of life drifted through my open window as the day went by, but I could not participate in any activity.

It's hard to remain in bed when others are engaged in daily activities with the accompanying laughter and fun. But Leah was determined to make me feel better, and after the other students had returned from dinner, she knocked on my door.

Entering with a tray of *tuwonbrabisco* and *miyankuka* soup, she said, "Hello C.A. How are you doing today?" She spoke to me in Hausa.

She called me "C.A." — the initials of my name, Comfort Ambrose. She had given me the nickname.

"Hello, Leah. I'm fine," I responded in Hausa, even though I felt ill. Making a cheerful return to a greeting is an expected cultural custom.

"Yayajikinki? Akwaisauki?" she asked ("How is your body now? Are you feeling better?")

"Da sauki," I replied ("I'm feeling better.)

I was grateful to see Leah. But I had no appetite for the food she brought, despite not eating anything all day. I left it untouched by the bedside.

"How was class today?" I asked, hoping to steer the conversation away from food.

"Same as always. You can borrow my notes when you're feeling better."

"Thank you, Leah," I said.

At mealtime, Leah always made sure to pray to God, thanking Him for His provision. This day was no different.

"Let's give thanks to God," she said.

We bowed our heads and Leah led us in prayer. "Almighty God," she said, "we thank You for giving us food. Bless it so that it can nourish our bodies. May You heal C.A. In Jesus' name, I pray. Amen."

"Amen," I echoed.

I glanced up at her. "What's the news?" I asked. "I heard some talk about a threatening letter arriving from Boko Haram." I remember asking her because I wanted reassurance that the talk wasn't true.

Leah hesitated, looking into the distance. "Who knows if they mean what they say? They could very well just be trying to scare us away from school."

So, a threatening letter had actually been delivered. *Hmm*, I thought, we could push it to the back of our minds and get on with our lives. But suppose the threat would be carried out? When Leah answered me, I sensed tension in her voice. Boko Haram was the most ruthless terrorist group in the world! Fear gripped me.

Leah must have sensed my fear. "Even if it's true," she said confidently, "we'll stand firm in our faith. God will watch over us. In any case, should you be worrying about that now? You need to take care of yourself and get some rest or I shall have to copy notes for you all week."

"I won't put you through such trouble all week long," I laughed.

Leah joined me in laughter. Her humor eased the tension.

A moment later, she said, "You know that God has given each of us different gifts. Some have the gift of teaching, some of preaching..." And she went on.

I took a handful of *tuwo* and ate as Leah talked. Hearing her preach was familiar and comforting.

Then suddenly a burst of gunshots shattered the air!

Leah stopped in mid-sentence. My heart pounded as we waited in silence, wondering if the gunshots would continue. Neither of us wanted to say aloud that we had heard gunfire, as if not saying it would somehow make it less true.

Finally, trying to be casual, Leah muttered, "Did you hear that?"

More gunshots rang out!

To this day, when I close my eyes I live out the following moments as though they happened only yesterday, as if I am living them out in the present.

Shouting arises in the distance.

I sit up. "We might be in trouble," I say.

"It sounds like gunfire," Leah says of what we now know for sure to be gunfire.

My shaking hands drop the *tuwo* back on the plate. Leah grabs me and prays, "Lord Jesus, please protect us." Her voice quivers. "Lord Jesus, *please protect us!*"

I tremble in my daze. It's happening. It's real. Something has to be done.

"Come on." I fumble out of bed. "Let's get out of here."

The running footsteps of other students thunder in the corridor. Leah grabs my hand and drags me toward the door.

"What's going on?" she yells to the other girls. "Were those gunshots?"

No one stops to answer. The only response is a confused shrug from a girl rushing past.

Leah takes charge. "Come on, we've got to get to the school gate!"

Everyone rushes toward the school gate. This is the agreed meeting point in case of trouble. Leah is protecting me in a firm grip as we make our way there.

More gunshots sound!

The firing is getting closer, and this causes more panic and confusion. Teachers emerge from the staff quarters to join us. They try to calm us down, but we can't be comforted.

Leah tells me, "Let me ask one of the teachers what's going on."
She hurries from my side.

As she leaves, vehicles roar round the bend, screeching toward us.
The vehicles are occupied by men armed with guns.

"Run!" someone screams from the crowd of girls and teachers.

The command sends everyone from the school into greater
pandemonium. Girls scatter in all directions. Some fall and are
trampled upon. I try to hurry away from the gate, but my body
is too weak. The adrenalin that had propelled me to the gate has
worn off.

My body is rebelling. I stoop over. I'm exhausted. I do not think I
can make it.

"C.A.!" A Christian friend named Mary calls. A group of students
rush past. Mary grabs my arm and points toward a fallen section of
the school fence. "Let's go that way!" she yells over the uproar.

I don't want to leave without Leah, but when I turn to look for her,
I cannot see her in the chaos. I find myself in Mary's tight grip. I
have no choice but to go with Mary, for I can do nothing in my
own strength. With her help, I manage to overcome the pain and
make it to the fence.

Mary easily scales the chest-high wall, but I can't even raise my
legs to climb. Mary reaches over and pulls me up. She lowers me
on the other side. We are on the other side — out of the large
school compound.

In the distance, we see men standing by a vehicle. We do not want
to be seen, so we move in and out of the bush, making our way
toward a road. Spotting an uncompleted building on the way, we
run to it. I am growing weaker by the second.

"Stop!" A voice bellows at us.

This command from the mouth of terror ignites my will to live. The bellow is followed by gunfire in our direction. We let go of each other and dart around the building. The structure shields us momentarily from the line of sight of the attackers.

We pause to catch our breath. We must keep running. But I cannot. I am exhausted. I shove Mary ahead. "Go!" I plead, knowing that we would both be caught if she stays with me.

Vehicles roar in our direction. They draw closer. I try to will myself to run, but my body won't cooperate. I am staggering. I won't make it. Mary is running. I am stumbling toward the tall grass on the side of the road. I need to run, but I can't.

I am done.

And then somehow, *I am saved!*

I trip on an unseen rock and fall headlong into a deep ditch. I tumble and roll, then come to a stop. I cower under tall grass blades, as the jeeps of terror round the bend. I hear voices close by, just behind me. I hold my breath and lie as still as I can. I try not to make a sound.

One jeep passes. Then I hear two. Three. I fear that my pounding heart will give me away. *Jesus, help me! Please, Jesus! Jesus! Jesus! Jesus! Please, Jesus! Please, help me!*

I hear a sound behind me. Someone is right behind! Two men – talking to each other.

"Where are all the Christian girls?" one of them asks another. "I thought they told us there were many Christian girls here. Did we come to the wrong school?"

I'm about to explode with fear. A vehicle revs up. The two men nearby shout to the drivers so they can jump on the vehicle. Feet pound on dirt, then on metal. Doors slam shut. The vehicle drives off.

The sounds of vehicle engines fill the air. Jeeps and trucks come and go. Engines. Engines. Then the engine sounds fade. Silence. A long silence. I let out a long breath and relax just a little. I am bruised from my fall. My skin is torn from the merciless thorns into which I plunged. Blood trickles down my arms from my wounds. Despite the pain, I'm extremely grateful that I'm undiscovered. I stay deathly quiet and don't move. I know they can still find me.

The sky is dark now and there is a chill in the air. When we fled in panic from the dormitories, I wore only a thin wrapper of fabric. The wrapper fell off in all the commotion. It's going to be a long, cold night for me in this ditch. But I'm rejoicing that I haven't been taken captive. "Thank you, Jesus," I say silently. "Thank you!"

I don't dare move till morning for fear of still being abducted. I don't dare make a sound.

As dawn arrives, I cautiously push myself up to look around. Behold, there at the other end of the ditch is Mary! She has been nearby all night, but neither of us realized it as we lay motionless through the long hours, petrified of being captured or killed.

Quietly I call her name and she turns. We're overjoyed to see each other. She helps me up, carefully plucking out the thorns all over me. We hug, astonished and grateful to be alive. Others arrive to help us.

The sheer terror of the experience is the other memory that clings to me. They are moments I do not want to relive, but they are part of my story. And they are part of Leah's story too. Leah — my compassionate and caring friend, my friend of friends who, in the face of unimaginable terror, stood angelically firm in her faith.

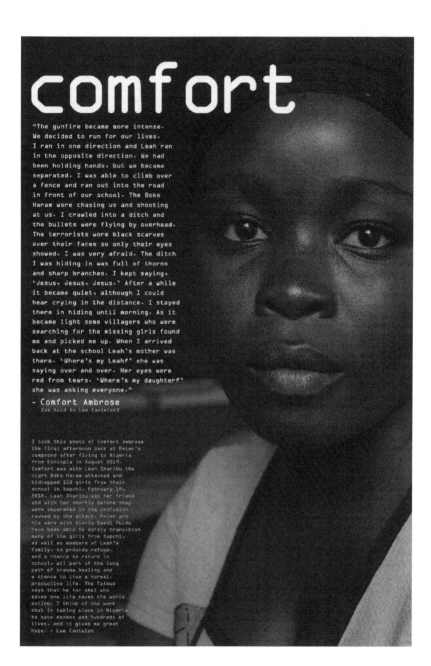

comfort

"The gunfire became more intense.
We decided to run for our lives.
I ran in one direction and Leah ran
in the opposite direction. We had
been holding hands, but we became
separated. I was able to climb over
a fence and ran out into the road
in front of our school. The Boko
Haram were chasing us and shooting
at us. I crawled into a ditch and
the bullets were flying by overhead.
The terrorists wore black scarves
over their faces so only their eyes
showed. I was very afraid. The ditch
I was hiding in was full of thorns
and sharp branches. I kept saying,
'Jesus, Jesus, Jesus.' After a while
it became quiet, although I could
hear crying in the distance. I stayed
there in hiding until morning. As it
became light some villagers who were
searching for the missing girls found
me and picked me up. When I arrived
back at the school Leah's mother was
there. 'Where's my Leah?' she was
saying over and over. Her eyes were
red from tears. 'Where's my daughter?'
she was asking everyone."

- Comfort Ambrose
  [as told to Lee Cantelon]

I took this photo of Comfort Ambrose
the first afternoon back at Peter's
compound after flying to Nigeria
from Ethiopia in August 2019.
Comfort was with Leah Sharibu the
night Boko Haram attacked and
kidnapped 110 girls from their
school in Dapchi, February 19,
2018. Leah Sharibu was her friend
and with her shortly before they
were separated in the confusion
caused by the attack. Peter and
his work with Gloria Saedi Puldu
have been able to safely transition
many of the girls from Dapchi,
as well as members of Leah's
family, to provide refuge,
and a chance to return to
school, all part of the long
path of trauma healing and
a chance to live a normal,
productive life. The Talmud
says that he (or she) who
saves one life saves the world
entire. I think of the work
that is taking place in Nigeria
to save dozens and hundreds of
lives, and it gives me great
hope. - Lee Cantelon

6

VASHTI'S ACCOUNT
Captured

I NEVER KNEW I WOULD COME FACE-TO-FACE WITH terrorists. I suppose no one really gives much thought to such a possibility in hopes that it will never happen. Drills can prepare us for the unthinkable. But the real test of how we'll respond only comes when the event we have prepared for actually happens.

When the attack from Boko Haram came, the wave of pandemonium carried me step by step — although in the wrong direction.

"Come this way!" a soldier commanded.

Men in Nigerian military uniforms motioned us to the many vehicles outside the gate. Amid the terror and confusion, this seemed to be our only way out. All other routes were blocked by masked men with guns. As I walked outside the gate, hope seemed tangible, as though appearing right in front of me. Ten vehicles lined up, and quickly filled with girls.

Leah grabbed my hand. "Vashti, let's get in," she said, as other girls scrambled in.

These men looked like soldiers, right? So surely we could trust them, couldn't we? I scrambled up the tailgate with the other frantic girls fighting their way inside.

Then suddenly...

Thud!

I hit the ground.

Knocked down from the vehicle!

The pain left me dazed. *Someone had pushed me out of the vehicle in order to get in!* Scrambling to my feet, I noticed that though the men wore military uniforms, they wore sandals and shoes on their feet instead of military boots. A chill ran through me. This was no rescue operation. These men were the terrorists!

"Leah, get out of the truck!" I screamed. "It's a trick! It's Boko Haram!"

The noise of confusion was so loud that I couldn't be heard. Worse, the engine of the truck started up, drowning out my pleas.

"No! No!" I yelled. *"No!"* But no one turned my way.

As the trucks drove away in a cloud of dust, I took to my heels. A man behind shouted at me to stop.

Stop?

I ran for dear life! Hearing the footsteps charging after me, I felt sure that I would be caught. Then a voice within me told me to hide behind a tree that loomed in front of me. As I did, the man ran right past, somehow failing to see me!

I waited behind the tree a long time until all others had gone. I heaved a great sigh of relief and cautiously made my way back to the school. There I discovered that many of the girls had been taken by the men.

To this day, I have no idea who pushed me out of the vehicle and how I somehow hid behind that tree without being seen. Some might call it luck, but I know that God protected me. I am so grateful to Him that I escaped.

Nevertheless, the thought continually nags at me that I walked away with only bruises, while Leah and many of the other girls suffered so greatly.

7

REBECCA'S ACCOUNT #2
Where Is My Daughter?

"They have taken the girls!"

NOTHING COULD PREPARE ME TO HEAR THOSE words. No mother should have to endure that kind of paralyzing heartache. Our biggest fear had been confirmed. The gunshots we heard had come from Boko Haram. The only information we received that night was that some of the girls had been kidnapped.

No one knew which girls or how many. The uncertainty led to inconsolable tears taking over my emotions and entire body. Was Leah hurt? Was she one of the girls taken? *Where was she?*

I called my husband, Nathan, stationed in Yola, Adamawa State, about eight hours away. We agreed that we would pray, trust God, and first thing in the morning I should investigate and call him with any news.

Throughout the night I sobbed out my prayers, pleading that my only daughter be kept safe. Many times I let my tears be my only prayer when my tongue could form no words. The only solace that dawn at last brought me was the fact that Boko Haram had vacated the area. We could now go to the school to search for Leah.

With the town awakening from its nightmare on a new day, parents by the score rushed to the school searching for their daughters. I clung to every hope I could muster that I would find Leah. But human hope is fragile.

One by one, girls emerged from their hiding places, finally realizing the terror had ended. Families all around erupted in joyous reunions. But Leah was not among the girls. My hope seemed to be turning to despair. Yet I battled on and focused on finding her.

I inquired about her from several girls that I recognized to be members of Leah's Christian Fellowship at school. However, none had seen her. My heart began to shudder, fearful of terrible news. Government soldiers arrived and endeavored to bring order to the chaos. Yet they could bring no order to my heart.

School officials decided to take a roll call for each class to see which girls were missing. Some of the girls acknowledged their presence when their names were called. Other names met with silence, including that of Leah. *Leah? No answer!* The deafening silence felt like a knife in my soul.

So many girls had been taken before, but the terror caused by Boko Haram had not been stopped. Had this atrocity not happened in Chibok? Now it had stormed our homes here in Dapchi to slay us. The threat had become real. The horror had fractured our lives.

The tally of missing girls amounted to 110 — an incomprehensible number. Too many families having to return home without their daughters. Including me.

Though I knew the truth in my heart, I could not accept that Boko Haram had my precious Leah in their clutches. *How could I?* They surely had taken her and I could do nothing about it. I felt utterly worthless. Somehow it seemed entirely my fault.

My friends and I then conducted our own private painstaking search. We beat the bushes, called out Leah's name, shouted ourselves hoarse — to no avail. Even Bulus, a dear family friend whose daughters had been feared taken, joined us in the search after discovering his daughters had been found safe. We continued the search.

But no matter how thoroughly we searched, how far and wide we looked, the fragile thread of hope faded into nothing. Leah was nowhere to be found. Finally, reality compelled us to slog our way back home. And we went without Leah. My thoughts kept returning again and again to my darling daughter. *What had happened to her? What had become of my precious one?*

Then the news arrived that some of the girls who had been injured during the invasion had been taken to a nearby hospital for treatment. *Hope!* Surely, Leah was among them? Hope again!

We hurried to the hospital. Would Leah be there? Would she be among the injured girls in the hospital now rejoicing with their arriving loved ones? I frantically looked everywhere, but I could not find her. My heart ached. I wanted to rejoice with those rejoicing, but I felt too devastated to do that. My heart was too broken.

Now, in addition to having to face the grim reality that Leah had been abducted by Boko Haram, I would have to face my husband.

Rebecca - Leah's Mother

Bulus and others had been in touch with him and relayed the tragic news. Nathan already had departed for home. How do you tell the loving father of your child that his only daughter has been snatched by the evil from which you were supposed to protect her?

We had tried as parents to do everything for our children. We tried to provide them with love, the essentials of life, godly training to prepare them for a good future. Had we done enough to protect them from the peril of inhumane terrorists?

I questioned everything we had done. I let thoughts flog and batter my mind. What happened to her? Why did this happen to us and why hadn't we moved away when the threats first came? Why? How could we have let this happen to our only daughter? How? How could God have not protected our Leah? We had prayed for protection, hadn't we? We had prayed fervently! Where was God when Boko Haram attacked?

Doubts about God kept creeping into my mind, but I quickly had to erase them. Hope in God is the constant people like us have left after the wickedness of the world snatches everything else away.

My husband returned to Dapchi that day and we began to fast and pray. We haven't stopped praying. We pray to God to protect Leah.

Nathan and Rebecca - Leah's Parents

We pray to God to use Leah in a mighty way. We pray to God to use her for the Gospel. We pray, we pray!

Leah turned out to be the only Christian student taken, the only one out of the 20 students who belonged to the school's Christian Fellowship. This cannot be a coincidence. Many of the other Christian girls have spectacular stories of God's providential deliverance that day. We pray that Leah's faith will stay strong to combat the evil around her. We pray that God will keep her. We pray that He will use her for His glory.

Sorrow ravages through me. *Where is my daughter?* I do not know the answer. We have prayed to God and asked questions of the government. To date we have answers from neither. How I pray to wake up from this never-ending nightmare!

Leah's Empty Room

8

BULUS'S ACCOUNT
The Girls Return

IN THE SPAN OF ONE MONTH, SO MUCH CHANGED IN Dapchi. My town lost the beat that once pounded its heart with liveliness. Instead, the mood became sad and depressed, with residents trying to come to terms with the terror that had visited us.

Relatives cried for their missing daughters. The families whose daughters had been spared could not really celebrate in the midst of the grief of those whose girls had vanished.

No one knew how to live anymore. Parents hardly let their children out to play for fear of further attacks. Instead of fun-loving communal gatherings that had defined our evenings, locals stayed in small groups, whispering about the incident. Although I worked as a police officer and therefore should have been able to help, I felt utterly helpless in the midst of all the unanswered questions.

When the girls had been in captivity for about a month, rumors circulated that they might soon be released. The buzz created a new hope. Soon, the specified day came and the whole town gathered.

Everyone waited in anticipation. I stood in the crowd, too, but not in my police uniform, for fear of standing out to Boko Haram. Leah's father, Nathan, had to once again depart for his police post in Yola, so I waited in his place with Rebecca and her older sister.

Long minutes dragged by and I prayed this would not be a hoax. The families had been through so much and had now been given a glimmer of hope. I prayed that their expectation would not be dashed once again. I especially wanted it to be real for the sake of the Sharibu family, my dear friends. Just when those gathered began to get edgy, the Boko Haram terrorists appeared and made their way toward the town center.

Boko Haram

They had covered their faces. They brandished weapons. The sight of this embodiment of sheer evil completely hushed the crowd. At first the men appeared to be alone, but soon the girls became visible. We were all relieved to see them, though we couldn't identify individuals because of the long outfits and brown hijabs they wore. Each girl had a number that labeled her.

The first of the girls released ran into the waiting arms of their families. A great celebration with much hugging and tears of joy followed. It seemed that the town of Dapchi, piece by piece, would be put back together. I stood by Rebecca and her sister, waiting with them for Leah.

Other parents who had not received their daughters back scanned the crowd for them. The tension brought questions. Where were the rest of the girls? I could not bear to watch as I saw hope dwindling in the eyes of my dear friends.

Behold, yet another set of girls came into view. And the girls, dressed and numbered like the ones before, and released in the same manner, ran into the arms of their loving relatives. Still, Leah didn't appear in this group. Rebecca looked all around. *Where was Leah?*

Frantically, Rebecca moved among the families, searching for her daughter. "Where is she, Lord?" I could hear her mutter. Grief, deep disappointment, tears, agony, all etched in her face. Her hope waned.

Amid the boisterous reunions, news came to me that a few of the girls had been dropped off at the chief of Dapchi's house. Without sparing a moment to tell Rebecca and her sister, I hurried off in that direction. I greatly anticipated reuniting Leah with her family!

At the chief's house, I received the disappointing news of Leah's absence. Yet, more stunning came the story recounted by some of the returned girls about what had happened to her.

How could I relay this development? How was I supposed to go back and tell Rebecca the shocking truth I had just discovered?

9

THE CAPTURED MUSLIM GIRLS' ACCOUNT
Great Respect

THE DAY OF THE TERRIBLE ATTACK WHEN GUNSHOTS rang out plummeted the whole school into chaos. In the confusion, men wearing military uniforms motioned us outside the school into waiting trucks. We never thought to question their intentions, certainly not at that moment.

In the ensuing panic we were overjoyed to think that soldiers wanted to get us to safety. No one suspected anything until we had been driven deep into the forest. Then the truth began to sink in: these men were actually Boko Haram terrorists. The realization came that it was too late to react. We had been taken captive!

Sambisa Forest

Crammed horribly in the trucks, we didn't dare protest for fear of being killed then and there. Five classmates suffocated to death from the intolerable condition of having to sit on top of each other. The men stopped in the forest and buried them in shallow graves. The agonizingly long journey continued, until we came to a river before being placed on a boat. Hoping it would be over, we still had to travel three whole days down a river before we finally arrived at the camp.

The men took us to a tent which served as the entrance to an underground house with many rooms. Nevertheless, we all had to be packed into just one large room. Our diet consisted primarily of plain boiled rice, with no stew, no spices, no salt, no oil. On a few occasions, we received poorly cooked *tuwobrabisco* and *kuka* soup.

This form of captivity continued for an entire month under terrible conditions. Every day we performed ablution (the ritual washing of our bodies) and prayed our Islamic prayers, which is a normal Muslim rite. This routine set Leah apart from all the other girls. Leah just sat and watched the rest of us. I surmise that she silently said her own Christian prayers.

When Boko Haram members realized that Leah didn't perform any of the rites, they asked her why. Leah boldly professed her Christianity. It may have been brave, but that obviously resulted in Leah becoming their target. Sure enough, the men hurried off to notify their leader.

The leader came marching in with an angry scowl on his face. He leaned toward Leah and demanded to know her name. Not only did Leah announce her name, but she declared her Christian faith. While she may have been scared — she had to have been — she didn't show it.

The leader became furious and threatened to kill her if she didn't renounce her Christianity by reciting the Islamic creed (*Kalmar Shahada*).

Leah refused.

Some of the captors then gave her a brutal beating, ordering her to renounce her faith in Jesus and to join Islam. Though Leah knew yielding would make them stop the beating, she refused to turn her back on Christianity. We pleaded with her to tell them what they wanted to hear, and even said we would recite the creed so she could voice it out to them, but she remained adamant.

When the men realized their brutality didn't compel a conversion, they stopped, seeming confused. After a while, they gathered together again to continue their punishment, this time beating her more mercilessly in the belief that it would force an acceptance of Islam.

It didn't work. Clearly Leah would never renounce her Christian beliefs just to be set free. In frustration, the abductors threw her into a small, dark room near the rest of us. The room resembled more of a cage than anything else.

At this point, Leah was separated from all the other girls who had been taken. This occurred the night before the rest of us returned home to be reunited with our families. Leah remained a prisoner because she held firmly to her Christian faith.

As we drove away the next morning, we heard her crying, pleading to be allowed to return home with us. Although we have religious beliefs different from hers, we have the greatest respect for this girl called Leah. She is a brave person!

We have not seen her since we separated, but it is with keen eagerness that we hope to see this special girl once again.

IO

REBECCA'S FINAL ACCOUNT
A Desire for My Leah

WHEN BOKO HARAM RETURNED TO THEIR ENCLAVE, we searched everywhere among the girls for Leah, but our dear daughter was nowhere to be found. Hearing that some of the girls had been dropped off at the town's health center, I ran there, followed by my elder sister and others. But Leah was not there.

We then learned some of the girls had been taken to the house of the chief of Dapchi. Frantic, I immediately started off. As I arrived at the house, I saw Bulus coming toward me with a grim look on his face. He and some of the girls who had been captured disclosed the news about my daughter. She had not been returned because she would not renounce her Christianity. She remained the only one still in captivity!

I tried to make sense of this devastating news. All hope seemed gone. Clearly no matter where we looked or how hard we tried, we would not find Leah. She was still being held by these evil men. As this realization overwhelmed me, I passed out. After being rushed to the health center, I revived, but I wept uncontrollably at the thought that Leah remained all alone in captivity.

Bulus stayed with me at the health center and calmed me down with strong words of encouragement. He began to recount to me how the testimonies of the eyewitnesses confirmed that Leah had bravely stood for Jesus and how it amazed the released girls that she had refused to renounce her faith. I sat stunned and confused, pondering how this could be. Bulus continued, "The Bible assures us that trials will come our way, but we must keep trusting the Lord and hoping for Leah's release. What she has done is to be tremendously commended. It is a great lesson that should make us all stand for our faith, as she has so heroically done."

Powerfully, a deep feeling of supernatural peace began to flow over me as Bulus spoke those words. I felt the Lord's presence around me and received a surge of strength to trust God anew and put the whole situation into His hands.

This may sound self-centered, but I must admit I never wanted my daughter to be a hero. I wanted to always have my Leah with me and for her to be back in my arms. I think that is the deep desire of any mother. What I wouldn't give to once again feel Leah's warm skin against mine and to breathe in her sweet scent! I don't want those senses to be just a fading memory.

God has given me the ability to love my children with a greater love than I could ever have imagined. He entrusted my children into my care. That is a great responsibility. I wanted them to grow into the persons that God wanted them to be. My greatest concern is that they should accept and live for Jesus.

Who could ever have imagined that the beautiful gift of salvation that my children would receive would lead to my own greatest trial? Now that I cannot see or fully understand God's greater purpose, I have to entrust my daughter into His care.

Already the incident has united both Muslims and Christians in Dapchi under one cause. This is all beyond my comprehension. I am exceedingly proud of my daughter's strength and resilience. How could I be otherwise? Nevertheless, as a mother, I still have my questions. Is she OK? Am I ever going to see her again? Why did it have to be her? Why couldn't she be released with everyone else?

Oh, how I long to have my daughter back safe and sound in my arms!

I cling to Psalm 18:2, which says, *"The LORD is my rock, my fortress, and my deliverer; my God is my rock, in whom I take refuge. He is my shield and the horn of my salvation, my stronghold."*

Only God's strength can help us prevail in the face of this continuing ordeal.

Each day our family has to remember the ultimate sacrifice that God made by sending his Son Jesus into the world to die on the Cross for our sins. God promises that in this world we will have trouble, but we must take heart because He has overcome the world.

Knowing all this doesn't mean that our days are not marked by heartache. But as we cling to the truth of God's love, which our friends have been sharing with us, we are reminded that this world is temporary and heaven is our real home. In heaven there is joy for those who have faith in God; no more tears, sorrow, suffering, or death. We long for heaven.

I am making Leah's story known, not because I have any pleasure in reliving it. No! I am making it known as a plea to the Nigerian government to make a serious effort to rescue my daughter, just as other girls were rescued. The government has made many promises, but to this day that hasn't resulted in action.

Telling her story is also my way of appealing to other Christians to pray for her release. We're grateful that her story has touched many lives around the world in ways we never thought possible. But I entreat her well-wishers to please continue to pray for her release and the release of so many other precious girls held in captivity.

Leah has been taken from us now for more than three years. We can't say for certain if she is alive or dead. A young lady who escaped from the terrorists sometime ago reported that Leah is still alive and had become something of a leader, giving hope and encouragement to others in captivity. Another young lady recently released also confirmed that Leah is still alive.

We are appealing to all who have heard about her kidnapping to join us in prayer. There is power in prayer! God works with prayer, and we need the help of others in the effort to have our Leah released.

Rebecca showing family photo

II

NATHAN & DONALD'S ACCOUNTS
Sorrow, Yet Hope!

Nathan

I MISS MY DAUGHTER LEAH SO MUCH! IT OFTEN HITS me hard in the early morning. I wonder if she is really gone, then comes the painful realization that it is true. My heart aches that she is still in captivity and that I can't rescue her from Boko Haram. I am her father and am supposed to protect her. So many thoughts swirl in my mind: where is she, what is she going through, why could we not protect her, why did God not protect her, will she be released?

I also struggle so much with thoughts of revenge against the terrorists who took her and are holding her. Truthfully, I often long for their deaths. Then I pray. Even for them somehow I find a path to forgiveness in my heart. I hope they repent and come to know Jesus. He is the only hope for these people. He is so much more powerful than they are, and by His might they will be defeated one day. Can some of them repent and come to Jesus? Although it seems impossible, all things are possible through our God, including the release of my precious Leah, in His time!

There have been many testimonials about Leah, but let me provide the perspective of her proud father.

Growing up, she was a good and respectful girl who did whatever I asked her to do, and with a good attitude. Whenever I or others would give her a task, we could be certain it would get done. Yet she was outspoken and strong-willed. Obviously, God used those strengths in her to stand up to the terrorists. She was also well-disciplined and did not concern herself with the worries of the world, like many of the girls in the village. Her yes was yes and her no was no. Leah never argued with me as her father, and the way she obeyed her parents and the Lord made us proud. We felt we had the kind of child that the Bible talks about (Psalm 127:3-5).

Leah exhibited great leadership qualities from an early age. She always helped her younger brother, Donald, and took good care of and protected him. She worked hard and always did her chores without complaining. In both primary and secondary school, she became the head girl. In her senior high school, she became the health prefect as well as being chosen the president of the Christian Fellowship.

She received the Lord at a young age and always enjoyed leading our family devotions at home. She loved Scripture and Bible stories.

Being far from my family because of my job resulted in me missing them all very much, so we spoke on the phone most every day. I always prayed for their safety, realizing the potential danger of Boko Haram operating in the general area. Because Leah and Donald's education was so important to us, we sacrificed so they could go to the best schools available. My wife did a great job taking care of our children, making it easier for me to be so far away. I have a wonderful wife and I love her greatly.

I received the terrible phone call from her the night of the attack when she told me she feared Boko Haram had entered Leah's school. Neither of us could sleep that night. We prayed and called each other several times to check for any updates.

I left early the next morning for Dapchi from Yola. It took several hours and the whole way I felt so anxious. My mind could not rest at all. As soon as I got to Dapchi, I rushed to my home to see my wife. So many people had filled our house. The women cried and the men consoled me, hoping Leah would be returned. My good friend Bulus offered great support. We are both from Adamawa State and served together as police officers in Dapchi, until my assignment to Yola. Our families have become close, and this incident has made us even closer.

In the midst of this trial, we do have hope Leah will be released. We so appreciate the Nigerians and others around the world — both Christians and Muslims — who are praying for her. I pray that this and other atrocities unite us to stand against the evil of terrorism. I also pray that one day Boko Haram will be defeated and all those in captivity will be released, in Jesus' name.

Donald

I MISS MY OLDER SISTER LEAH SO MUCH. SHE WAS MY sister, but also my friend. She took care of me, corrected me, helped me in school and in life. She had my back and watched out for me. I felt so safe in her presence. Her involvement in church and love of the Bible and Jesus provided a great example to me in my faith.

We played often together and especially loved to play a game called Lebo. Whenever I see others play that now, I get so sad and just start crying. I can't help it. The tears just come out.
On the day after the attack, I heard about it at the secondary school I attended. Our teachers gathered us and told us that Boko Haram had attacked Dapchi and had abducted some of the girls. My heart sank. I called my mother to check on Leah. I immediately sensed sadness in my mother's voice and then I knew. She told me that my sister had been taken. I burst into tears. My sadness has not diminished. I want my sister back home.

I turned 13 years old the day before the tragedy. I have often thought of what I will say to her when she returns and have practiced that in my mind. I will run and hug her and hold her in my arms and cry.

It has been hard without Leah, but I still have hope and pray for her release all the time. I know that God is good, even though bad things happen.

I want young people in Nigeria and around the world to know they can make a difference in this life. They are the leaders of tomorrow and can make a big impact today. No matter what the situation, never lose faith in God. Let Leah be an example to us all. No matter what happens or how hard life becomes, never deny Jesus and always cling to Him.

When I graduate from secondary school, I hope to be able to study and become a lawyer so I can stand up for the rights of people in my country Nigeria. I want to be like my sister, Leah, and make a real difference in this life!

12

GLORIA'S QUESTION
What is God Doing?

I HAVE OFTEN ASKED MYSELF, WHAT IS GOD DOING IN this seemingly terrible trial? Leah was taken at the young age of 14. She has been in captivity for more than three years and four birthdays.

God promises that all things work together for the good of those who love Him (Romans 8:28). He doesn't promise that we will always know how He works those things together for good. But here are some ideas that I have about this:

- Satan came to steal, kill, and destroy (John 10:10) and he meant this all for evil, but I can see how God is using it for good! (Genesis 50:20)

- Leah has become a hero to the nation of Nigeria and is now known in many other parts of the world.

- Her example has challenged millions of people to stand for Jesus in the face of persecution.

- She was specially chosen for this assignment by God. This is so evident by her state of readiness at the time of abduction. Note how all the other Christian girls escaped captivity that day, except her.

- The LEAH Foundation (Leah-Foundation.org), which started in her honor, has been used by God to care for her parents; her brother, Donald; her best friends who were also attacked that day; as well many other girls and women in distress due to some form of abuse (captivity).

- Additionally, Leah's story has opened doors for the reality of Christian persecution in Nigeria to be made known abroad. For  instance, as a result of an invitation from U.S. Vice President Mike Pence, Leah's mother, Rebecca, and I had the opportunity to testify in Washington, D.C. before congressional representatives about religious persecution in Nigeria.

- The U.S. Commission on International Religious Freedom placed Nigeria 12th on its watchlist and designated Leah as a prisoner of conscience.

- We had prayer meetings with influencers such as U.S. Sen. Ted Cruz and Tony Perkins, chairman of the U.S. Commission for International Religious Freedom.

- We held a "Global Prayer Vigil" on the steps of the U.S. Capitol with American leaders.

- We made two trips to Washington, D.C. and one to London to meet with world leaders to mark Leah's two years in captivity, a privilege only God can give to ordinary people like us (Matthew 10:18).

- The United Kingdom trip allowed us to meet with parliamentarians of both the House of Lords and House of Commons, resulting in the 2020 All-Party Parliamentary Group Religious Freedom Report being dedicated to Leah as the Face of Those Persecuted for Their Faith Globally.

Rebecca and Gloria at the Rally in London

What is God doing in this? I don't fully know, but I do know that God is good and that He is in control and will turn what Satan meant for evil into good. God holds Leah in His mighty hand!

Now I ask: Will you stand for God in the face of persecution or death? Do you know Him and know that He will work all things together for your good? He loves you so much! There is a world out there dying without Jesus and without hope.

Will you pray for Leah and others like her in captivity? Will you also pray that through Leah's testimony people of all nations might be challenged to boldly live out their faith in Jesus?

In the midst of hard times, let's choose to stand courageously for the Lord as Leah has. As we do, He will certainly use us to change the world around us.

Rebecca with the Archbishop of Canterbury and his wife, Caroline.

Rebecca and Gloria Samdi-Puldu met with the Archbishop of Canterbury and attended a special prayer meeting at his invitation. Afterward, they went to his office and he prayed for them again.

13

PETER'S PLEA
Come to Know God Personally Like Leah

A S WE ARE INSPIRED BY LEAH'S STORY, SHE BECOMES A hero to us all. But more importantly, her story points us to the ultimate hero, Jesus Christ. As she lives in captivity, she is actually free because she knows God personally and she knows that when she dies, she will be in heaven with Jesus.

Can you say the same for yourself?   Please carefully consider the following:

What does it take to begin a relationship with God? Do you need to devote yourself to unselfish religious deeds? Must you become a better person so that God will accept you?

You may be surprised that those actions won't work. But God has made it very clear in the Bible how we can know Him.

The following principles will explain how you can personally begin a relationship with God, right now, through Jesus Christ.

PRINCIPLE 1

God loves you and offers a wonderful plan for your life.

GOD'S LOVE
"God so loved the world that He gave His one and only Son, that whoever believes in Him shall not perish, but have eternal life" (John 3:16).

GOD'S PLAN
Jesus said, *"I came that they might have life, and might have it abundantly"* (John 10:10) — that is, that life might be full and meaningful.

> Why is it that most people are not experiencing the abundant life? Because ...

———

PRINCIPLE 2

All of us sin, and our sin has separated us from God.

WE ARE SINFUL
"All have sinned and fall short of the glory of God" (Romans 3:23).

We were created to have fellowship with God, but because of our stubborn self-will, we chose to go our own way, and our fellowship with God was broken. This self-will, characterized by an attitude of active rebellion or passive indifference, is what the Bible calls sin.

WE ARE SEPARATED

"The wages of sin is death" (Romans 6:23). Death is spiritual separation from God.

God is holy and people are sinful. A great gulf separates us. We are continually trying to reach God and the abundant life through our own efforts, such as living a good life, philosophy, or religion – but we inevitably fail.

The third principle explains the only way to bridge this gulf.

———

PRINCIPLE 3

Jesus Christ is God's only provision for our sin. Through Him we can know and experience God's love and plan for our lives.

HE DIED IN OUR PLACE

"God demonstrates His own love toward us, in that while we were yet sinners, Christ died for us" (Romans 5:8).

HE ROSE FROM THE DEAD

"Christ died for our sins ... He was buried ... He was raised on the third day, according to the Scriptures ... He appeared to Peter, then to the twelve. After that He appeared to more than five hundred" (1 Corinthians 15:3-6).

HE IS THE ONLY WAY TO GOD

"Jesus said to him, 'I am the way, and the truth, and the life; no one comes to the Father, but through Me'" (John 14:6).

God has bridged the gulf that separates us from Him by sending His Son, Jesus Christ, to die on the Cross in our place to pay the penalty for our sins.

It is not enough just to know these three principles ...

PRINCIPLE 4

We must individually receive Jesus Christ as Savior and Lord; then we can know and experience God's love and plan for our lives.

WE MUST RECEIVE CHRIST

"As many as received Him, to them He gave the right to become children of God, even to those who believe in His name" (John 1:12).

WE RECEIVE CHRIST THROUGH FAITH

"By grace you have been saved through faith; and that not of yourselves, it is the gift of God; not as a result of works, that no one should boast" (Ephesians 2:8-9).

When we receive Christ, we experience a new birth.

WE RECEIVE CHRIST BY PERSONAL INVITATION

Jesus says, *"Behold, I stand at the door and knock; if anyone hears My voice and opens the door, I will come in to him"* (Revelation 3:20).

Receiving Christ involves turning to God from self (repentance) and trusting Christ to come into our lives to forgive our sins and to make us what He wants us to be. Just to agree intellectually that Jesus Christ is the Son of God and that He died on the Cross for your sins is not enough. Nor is it enough to have an emotional experience. You receive Jesus Christ by faith, as an act of the will.

Which circle would you like to have represent your life?

SELF-DIRECTED LIFE
You are in control and Jesus has no influence in your life. People like this have never received Jesus into their lives. They remain guilty and cut off from God by their sin.

CHRIST-DIRECTED LIFE
Jesus is in control and you are following Him as Lord. These people have received Jesus into their lives. They have been forgiven and experience God's love.

You can receive Christ right now by faith through prayer.

Prayer is talking to God. God knows your heart and is not as concerned with your words as He is with the attitude of your heart.

The following is a suggested prayer. If this prayer expresses the desire of your heart, then you can pray this prayer right now and Christ will come into your life, as He promised.

"Lord Jesus, I need You. Thank You for dying on the Cross for my sins. I open the door of my life and receive You as my Savior and Lord. Thank You for forgiving my sins and giving me eternal life. Take control of the throne of my life. Make me the kind of person You want me to be."

Find the four spiritual laws and additional resources at CRU.org
(Used with permission by GCM Nigeria)

Rebecca and Gloria with Becca Lubbert (USA) at press conference.
Becca was one of those who helped develop the LEAH Foundation.

Nathan, Donald and Rebecca Speak Out

THE DAPCHI GIRLS

grace abounds much more

Their story is the stuff nightmares are made of, full of blood, cries for mercy, tears, and of the innocence of youth being torn from them by violent and evil oppressors. Theirs is the too often repeated story of men wielding violence against their helpless victims, women and young girls. The night Leah Sharibu was taken hostage, they were with her. More than one hundred of their classmates and friends were kidnapped on that unimaginable February night in Dapchi in 2018. Leah is the only one of "the Dapchi girls," who remains captive. She is one of the focuses of Gloria Samdi Puldu's **Free Leah** movement. The other is to rebuild the lives and hopes of the surviving Dapchi girls. In their obscurity they represent the more than 10,000 young lives who are being held hostage today in Northern Nigeria. Replacing despair and trauma with optimism and healing is the twenty-four-seven work that calls us to abandon complacency, to see the world as it is but to also see it as it could be, by God's mighty grace.

photo: (Gloria Samdi Puldu (at right) with some of of the Dapchi girls, January 2020.

Lee Cantelon (Microboard) with Rebecca and Gloria in the U.S.

HUMAN
RIGHTS
WATCH

Boko Haram
continues to
prey on women
and girls as
spoils of war...

HUMAN RIGHTS WATCH APRIL 2019

Who will speak up for these little ones? **Helpless and half-abandoned. They've got the right to choose life they don't want to lose.** I've got to speak up, won't you? **Their precious lives are on the line. How can we be rid of them? Pay the cost and turn about, and face the young defendants. - Phil Keaggy (Little Ones)**

photograph January 2020 by Lee Cantelon

TRIBUTES TO LEAH

W E ARE IN AWE OF HOW MANY DIFFERENT influencers from around the world have been impacted by Leah and written tributes to her. Here are just a few:

Tony Perkins, vice chair, U.S. Commission for International Freedom, and president of the Family Research Council

Leah Sharibu has spent over three years in captivity. Boko Haram abducted her in 2018 and hasn't released her because she refuses to renounce her faith. The Nigerian government needs to be doing more to protect the freedom of religion, particularly in the northeast region. Over three years after [they] abducted Leah Sharibu, it is unacceptable to see the group continue to inflict such devastation on the Nigerian people. We are praying and working for her release. We will keep fighting for religious freedom in Nigeria.
— Press Release/Statements 11.2020
(from https://www.baptistpress.com/resource-library/news/with-hundreds-of-christians-killed-in-nigeria-in-june-uscirf-urges-nigerian-government-to-intervene/)

John Stonestreet, president, the Chuck Colson Center

The last time the world heard from Leah, she begged to be "treated with compassion" and asked "the government, particularly the president, to pity me and get me out of this serious situation." Three years later, Leah remains a prisoner, a "captive for Christ." Leah's case is only one example of the kind of violence and oppression Nigerian Christians face every day, especially in the country's mostly Muslim north. For years, Boko Haram and Muslim Fulani militants have killed, raped, kidnapped, and sought to "cleanse" parts of northern Nigeria of its Christian population. The LEAH Foundation is also working to establish places where girls like Leah can, when released, find a home, provisions, and an education. Named for the young girl still held by Boko Haram, "LEAH" is an acronym that stands for "Leadership," "Empowerment," "Advocacy," and "Humanitarian." This advocacy for girls like Leah and others who have been attacked and/or kidnapped by groups like Boko Haram is incredibly important. But first, Leah must be freed.

— Breakpoint.org press release on 2.4.21
(from https://breakpoint.org/three-years-is-too-long/)

Fiona Bruce, U.K. member of Parliament and prime minister's special envoy on Freedom of Religion or Belief

I make no apology for raising once again the plight of Leah Sharibu, whose mother, Rebecca, I met earlier this year. The sadness in Rebecca's eyes lives with me today, and my heart goes out to her. Leah was just 14 when she

was among the 110 school girls abducted by Boko Haram from their school. She is the only one still in captivity, because she has refused to renounce her Christian faith. She is now 17. I ask the minister once again, as I have done before, to ensure that Leah's plight, together with requests for her release, is raised with the Nigerian government at every possible opportunity.

— UK Parliament House of Commons 11.26.20

Baroness Caroline Cox, U.K. House of Lords

In the Parliament, I can be a voice as I use my position to speak out on behalf of those persecuted and vulnerable. We share in the suffering and grieve with the Sharibu family. We will continue to do all we can to help Leah. We will never give up. Leah represents the worldwide struggle both for freedom of religion and belief but also the unacceptable violence against women and girls. Sadly, there are thousands of girls in Nigeria and across the world. Leah needs each and every one of us to speak the truth about what is happening in Nigeria. The severity and scale of persecution is, at times, overwhelming and we don't always know how best to respond. But the longer we tolerate these massacres, abductions and atrocities, the more we emboldened the perpetrators. We call on all foreign governments and partners, and the Nigeria government, to commit to achieve Leah's return. Her example of faith, resilience and refusal to convert from Christianity to Islam and to suffer horrendous consequences is profoundly humbling. We are inspired and encouraged by Leah and it is a privilege to stand with the Sharibu family. We will never give up.

— From ICON/LEAH prayer event 2.19.21
(from https://www.youtube.com/watch?v=untT40-XdHQ)

U.S. Sen. Marco Rubio (Republican, Florida)

For three years Leah Sharibu has been held hostage by Boko Haram for refusing to renounce her Christian faith. She's the

only remaining victim abducted by the terrorist group in the 2018 Dapchi school kidnapping. The Nigerian government must ensure her safe release. #ExpressionNotOppression
— Twitter @MarcoRubio 2.19.21

U.S. Sen. Ted Cruz (Republican, Texas)

Leah is a Christian who refuses to renounce her faith and convert to Islam. That's why she is still being held hostage by Boko Haram. **Leah has said that she would rather live free in captivity, than live in freedom as a captive.** Those are remarkable, courageous words. For a young girl, facing a threat of her very life, they are extraordinary words of strength, and maturity, and hope. For days, months and years, Leah has been living in hellish captivity ... imagine what Leah is facing right now. As a parent of daughters, I can only imagine the agony Leah's family endures. My wife, Heidi, lived in Nigeria as a little girl, and, in Kenya when her parents were missionaries in both countries. I can't imagine Leah's strength ... in the face of evil Leah has demonstrated, and is demonstrating tremendous courage. I want to commend every voice here to be heard from the mountain tops. To be heard across the nation and across the globe. And I look forward to the day, hopefully very, very soon, where we can welcome Leah as free, liberated, and a powerful, powerful testimony for the love of Jesus Christ. God bless you."

(from https://www.cruz.senate.gov/?p=press_releaseandid=4730)

U.S. Senate

Senate Resolution 170: Calls for the immediate release of all Boko Haram captives, specifically the remaining Chibok schoolgirls and Leah Sharibu. The resolution also urges both Nigeria and the United States to take certain actions to address the abduction of women by Boko Haram.

- Bill sponsor: U.S. Sen. Tammy Baldwin (Democrat, Wisconsin)
- Bill co-sponsors: U.S. Senators Marco Rubio (Republican, Florida), Richard J. Durbin (Democrat, Illinois), Susan Collins (Republican, Maine), Jeanne Shaheen (Democrat, New Hampshire), Richard Blumenthal (Democrat, Connecticut)

(from https://projects.propublica.org/represent/bills/search?q=sharibu)

See also: **Bipartisan/Bicameral Letter calling for Leah Sharibu's Release** https://www.cruz.senate.gov/files/documents/Letters/2019.10.23_ Congressional%20Leah%20Sharibu%20Final%202019.pdf

Benjamin Watson, former NFL star and author

We in the USA seem to be largely unaware of the genocide that still rages in Nigeria. As we advocate for justice in America, we must not forget that justice is desperately needed outside of America as well. As I heard about Leah Sharibu, I was saddened to hear the news and I began to pray for her and her family. Even across the ocean and in an entirely different culture, she became a hero to me as her faith compelled her to stand for Christ, in the midst of unfettered persecution. We pray for her freedom and deliverance, but also that her spirit be renewed daily. I want to use the voice God gave me to stand with my brothers and sisters around the world and in Nigeria, to pray for her safety, health, and her release. We must speak up until the world hears us and governments are moved to intervene. In our daily lives, we can't forget the suffering of the body of Christ around the globe and realize that at some point we might be in a similar circumstance as Leah. How would we hope that they would react for us? The time is now, we cannot continue to be silent.

— From ICON/LEAH Prayer Event. 2.19.21
(from https://www.youtube.com/watch?v=untT4o-XdHQ)

Brent Theobald, former U.S. Marine Commander, Strategic Operations and director of Integritas

Our hearts break for Leah and her family. Hebrews 13:3 tells us to "Remember those imprisoned, as if you were there yourself. Remember also those being mistreated, as if you felt their pain in your own bodies." This is extremely convicting to me because so often we hear these heartbreaking stories, but compartmentalize them as "someone else" or "over there." I have two young daughters, and I must ask myself, what I would do differently if this was my own daughter? Would we not put all of our resources toward finding our own child and returning her home? May the Lord give us the ability to see Leah as He does, and may we have the strength and courage to pray, respond, and give to see her released.

Wole Soyinka, Nigerian playwright

I was quite impressed with what I saw in that young girl, Leah Sharibu, who told her abductors that: "No, you can't take away from me, my freedom." I saw in her the spirit of Kudirat Abiola, when she said No, she spoke for all of us. (June 5, 2018)

Odion Ighalo, former Manchester United and Nigerian professional footballer

It's been three years. I join [everyone] to say, free Leah Sharibu!

Peter Oboh Oboh, British Nigerian boxer and former World Boxing Association Intercontinental Lightweight Champion

I want both Nigerian Christians and Muslims to know that there is power in prayer. We should all pray for the young girl, Leah, for whom my heart is moved with compassion. We must pray for her immediate release as there is nothing God cannot do. With God on the side of His children, the immediate release of little Leah from her captors will soon be a thing of the past. We should all pray for her.

Yemi Osinbajo, Nigerian vice president

Because she refused to renounce Christianity, she will soon regain her freedom by virtue of her faith in the cross and the death of Jesus Christ (April 3, 2018).

Fani-Kayode, Nigerian politician

Leah Sharibu, deeply courageous, greatest Christian hero in Nigeria. She should be treated as a hero for standing her ground even at the point of death.

https://www.vanguardngr.com/2020/12/leah-sharibu-deeply-courageous-greatest-christian-hero-in-nigeria-fani-kayode-slams-garba-shehu/

McPhilips Elisha, director of Evangelical Missionary Society (the largest indigenous mission in Africa)

Leah has shown me courage in the face of death and brought alive the impact of true discipleship and teaching. I am forever impacted by her extravagant demonstration of faith — she is a faith checker for all of us who have come to place our faith in Christ, in a hostile society like ours.

Ambassador Rhoda Goodwill Jahota, chairperson, Women Wing of Christian Association of Nigeria

Leah is a strong and courageous girl who refused to compromise her faith. Her example has moved me to be brave and to encourage my children to be strong in the Lord.

Matt Redman, Christian musician

I want to add my voice of support to Leah and her family, and to all those who are working to obtain her release. What an amazing worshipper she is and what an amazing example of someone who has stuck to their beliefs, their faith and their worship for the name of Christ.

(https://www.youtube.com/watch?v=GVDZBsP_Ffc)

Caitlin Theobald, executive director, Give Her Voice

Leah's story is a modern-day equivalent of Esther. In one singular moment, all of her rights were stripped away. Her right to freedom. Her right to a happy childhood. Her right to pursue her dreams. Her right to marry and have a family. Her right to live. Abducted and imprisoned at age 14, she could have those rights back if only she would simply deny Jesus and convert to Islam. Deeply in love with Jesus, this girl already knew those rights died at the foot of the Cross. Like Queen Esther of old, she inspires and challenges us through her testimony with the simple phrase, "If I perish, I perish." She does this because she knows that this world is not her home, and these brief and temporary sufferings are nothing compared to the worth of knowing Jesus. Our family prays daily for Leah's protection and release. While we wait, her story strengthens our faith and she is a hero to all of us, but especially to my two young daughters. They often say, "If she can stand for Jesus, I can, too!"

Beth Kaura, Giving University (USA) coordinator

When I consider the life of Leah, I see a parallel to Daniel when he was in King Darius's court. Darius agreed to "an edict and enforce the decree that anyone who prays to any god or human being during the next 30 days, except to you, Your Majesty, shall be thrown into the lions' den." Daniel, of course, remained committed to God and prayed just as he had always done. Leah is in the lions' den, but she is not alone. Nor are any of us who are wounded, lost, impoverished, or desperate. I pray for her time in the "den," that this time of imprisonment is filled with the presence of the Lord, over and over again. And that people will be reminded of the steadfastness of His love for us (Daniel 6:7-21).

Kyle Abts, executive director, International Committee On Nigeria

Leah Sharibu, as a young Christian student, refused to forcibly convert to Islam, thus expressing her basic right of freedom of religion. Her choice of religion is legally protected, thus allowing her to worship in whatever manner she chooses and also share her faith peaceably with anyone she chooses. As a minor, Leah Sharibu was forcibly separated from her parents against their will, thus violating her fundamental human rights. This is also a violation of international significance as it hints at child/ human trafficking. Yet, it is sufficiently clear that as a domestic problem it is significant because the Constitution of the Federal Republic of Nigeria (1999) chapter II, section 17, item 3, subset f, states, "Children [and] young persons are protected against any exploitation whatsoever, and against moral and material neglect." If Nigeria claims to promote and support freedom of religion, then Leah Sharibu's situation should be examined and garrisoned.

If Nigeria claims to protect the rights of women and children, then Leah's issue should be front and center. If Nigeria is to be considered a democratic government and an ally to international partners, then accountability and impunity must cease. Leah Sharibu epitomizes the problems and concerns in Nigeria. If the Nigerian government is serious about rule of law, peace, and justice, they will do all they can to get Leah Sharibu released.

http://www.nigeria-law.org/ConstitutionOfTheFederalRepublicOfNigeria.htm#HighCourtOfFCTAbuja

Randy Matthews, director of Leadership Development, New Foundations International

When I think of modern Christian heroes, Leah Sharibu is in the top tier with the Hebrews 11 people "of whom the world was not worthy" (verse 38). These were ordinary people with an extraordinary faith, women and men who faced imprisonment and persecution because of their trust in the Lord, a people who refused to accept release if it meant compromising their faith. Leah has joined these who in ages past would not renounce their faith to be returned to their homes.

And what does this do to people like me? It melts away my inhibitions and motivates me to press on to hard places for God. Leah's courage, at such a young age, has inspired my faith, and when I share her story, others stand up for Christ with newfound confidence. Praying for her fuels my faith, even though she has not yet been freed, because I know that these prayers will fill her (and us) with boldness in bad times (Acts 4:24-31).

But her story does not stop with me or those around me. Leah's story is a bold encouragement to those in far off places who face the same kind of suffering. When someone persecuted in China hears of her, does it fill him or her with fresh wind and fire from the Holy Spirit? I wonder if anyone in Myanmar finds faith for one more day when they hear of Leah's days and years without release?

I cannot know what impact she has beyond my own heart and circle, but I rest assured that wherever her story is told, someone is filled with new hope in Jesus.

So now my prayer for Leah, and maybe your prayer, too, is found in this paraphrase of Psalm 71:1-5:

In you, O LORD, does Leah take refuge;

let her never be put to shame!

In your righteousness deliver her and rescue her;

incline your ear to her and save her!

Be to her a rock of refuge,

to which she may continually come;

you have given the command to save her,

for you are her rock and her fortress.

Rescue her, O God, from the hand of the wicked,

from the grasp of the unjust and cruel man.

For you, O LORD, are Leah's hope,

her trust, O LORD, from her youth.

ABOUT THE ARTIST

SINCE GRADUATING FROM LONDON'S PRESTIGIOUS Camberwell School of Art, painter David Goatley has gone on to become one of the most recognized portraitist in the world today. His more than 400 commissions include members of the British royal family, the maharaja of Jaipur, bishops, prime ministers, and well- known figures from academic, arts, and government fields.

In the summer of 2018, David felt moved to paint a portrait of Leah Sharibu after learning about her abduction from those who are working to assist her and for her release. As Leah Sharibu became "the face" of a sorrowful and ongoing crisis, this painting and the courage it represents has the potential to inspire many to work for justice, believe in God's power to change lives, and to take a stand for righteousness. "Paintings have the power to convey life and speak to the heart," David has said about his work, "and it is my sincere prayer that my portrait of Leah will motivate people to pray and work on her behalf."

For more information about the artist visit:
www.davidgoately.com

HOW *YOU* CAN HELP

Get Involved Now
Nothing you have not given away will ever be truly yours.

Learn more and give to girls like Leah at
Leah-Foundation.org

ABOUT THE AUTHORS

Dr. Gloria Samdi-Puldu hails from Adamawa State in northeastern Nigeria. She is married with three children.

She is currently the global director of Give Her Voice and president of the LEAH Foundation.

As a woman passionate about the sanctity of human life, she continually seeks to contribute to the empowerment of women and girls through opportunities that God brings her way. This passion leads her to be an advocate for the plight of persecuted and vulnerable women and girls across Africa.

She has an academic background, holding a doctorate in Political Science from the University of Ibadan, a Master of Science in International Relations and Strategic Studies, and a Bachelor of Science in Political Science, both from the University of Jos.

Gloria is also an educator with interest in research, and has written many publications and given numerous lectures at the University of Jos in the Department of Political Science.

Peter Fretheim grew up in a privileged life in Greenwich, Connecticut, just outside of New York City. His father was a multimillionaire and, although his family had everything the world has to offer, they did not have Jesus.

He became a believer in the Bible and true Christianity at the age of 16, then earned a Business Degree from Pepperdine University in California and started to work in business in the United States.

He felt God's calling and left business for the ministry and attended Dallas Theological Seminary, where he met his wife, Miriam. They both obtained Master's Degrees in Biblical Studies. They have lived in Nigeria since 1999, and raised their four children there. They love Nigeria and Nigerians, and hope to live there for many years to come.

Peter says, *"I don't own all of those fancy things I had growing up, but I now have true riches in Jesus."*

Made in the USA
Columbia, SC
24 December 2021

52620989R00054